SYMBOLS OF AME

The Liberty Bell

by Kirsten Chang

BELLWETHER MEDIA · MINNEAPOLIS, MN

Note to Librarians, Teachers, and Parents:

Blastoff! Readers are carefully developed by literacy experts and combine standards-based content with developmentally appropriate text.

Level 1 provides the most support through repetition of high-frequency words, light text, predictable sentence patterns, and strong visual support.

Level 2 offers early readers a bit more challenge through varied simple sentences, increased text load, and less repetition of high-frequency words.

Level 3 advances early-fluent readers toward fluency through increased text and concept load, less reliance on visuals, longer sentences, and more literary language.

Level 4 builds reading stamina by providing more text per page, increased use of punctuation, greater variation in sentence patterns, and increasingly challenging vocabulary.

Level 5 encourages children to move from "learning to read" to "reading to learn" by providing even more text, varied writing styles, and less familiar topics.

Whichever book is right for your reader, Blastoff! Readers are the perfect books to build confidence and encourage a love of reading that will last a lifetime!

This edition first published in 2019 by Bellwether Media, Inc.

No part of this publication may be reproduced in whole or in part without written permission of the publisher. For information regarding permission, write to Bellwether Media, Inc., Attention: Permissions Department, 6012 Blue Circle Drive, Minnetonka, MN 55343.

Library of Congress Cataloging-in-Publication Data

Names: Chang, Kirsten, author.
Title: The Liberty Bell / by Kirsten Chang.
Description: Minneapolis, MN : Bellwether Media, Inc., 2019. | Series:
   Blastoff! Readers: Symbols of American Freedom | Includes bibliographical references and index.
Identifiers: LCCN 2017061638 (print) | LCCN 2017061739 (ebook) | ISBN 9781626178847
   (hardcover : alk. paper) | ISBN 9781618914705 (pbk. : alk. paper) | ISBN 9781681035475 (ebook)
Subjects: LCSH: Liberty Bell–Juvenile literature. | Philadelphia (Pa.)–Buildings, structures, etc.–Juvenile literature.
Classification: LCC F158.8.I3 (ebook) | LCC F158.8.I3 C52 2019 (print) | DDC 974.8/11–dc23
LC record available at https://lccn.loc.gov/2017061638

Editor: Rebecca Sabelko   Designer: Andrea Schneider

Printed in the United States of America, North Mankato, MN.

Table of **Contents**

What Is the Liberty Bell?

The Liberty Bell is an American **symbol** for **freedom**.
It is in Philadelphia.

4

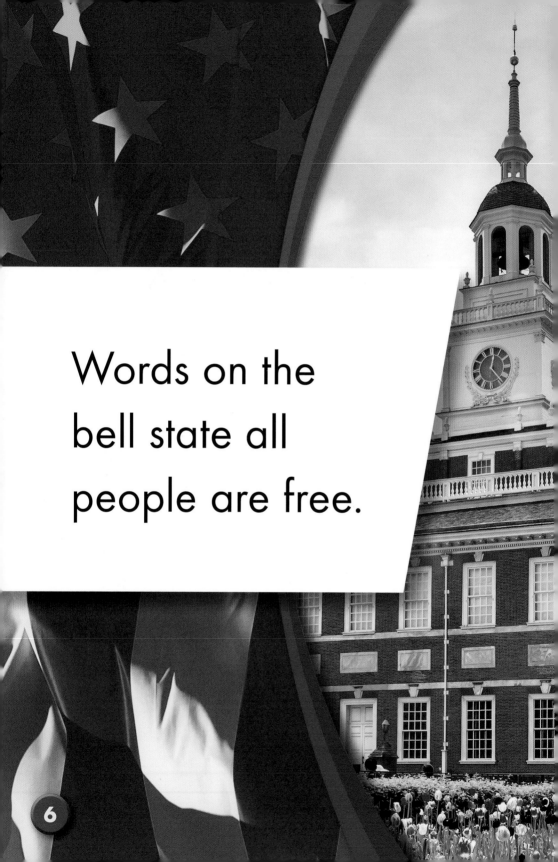

Words on the
bell state all
people are free.

Parts of the Liberty Bell

yoke

message

crack

clapper

The bell has a
crack. It does not
ring anymore.

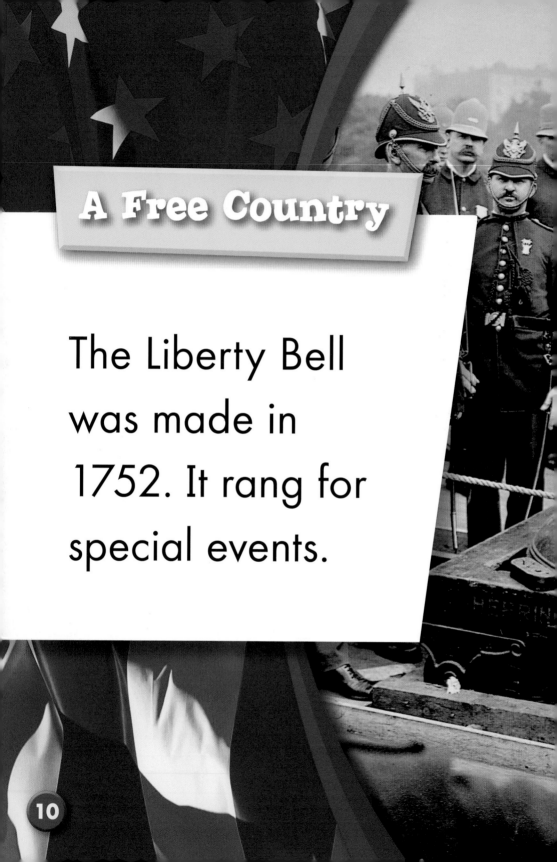

A Free Country

The Liberty Bell was made in 1752. It rang for special events.

There is a **legend** it rang in 1776. The sound stood for America's freedom.

Freedom for All

Long ago, it was called the State House Bell.

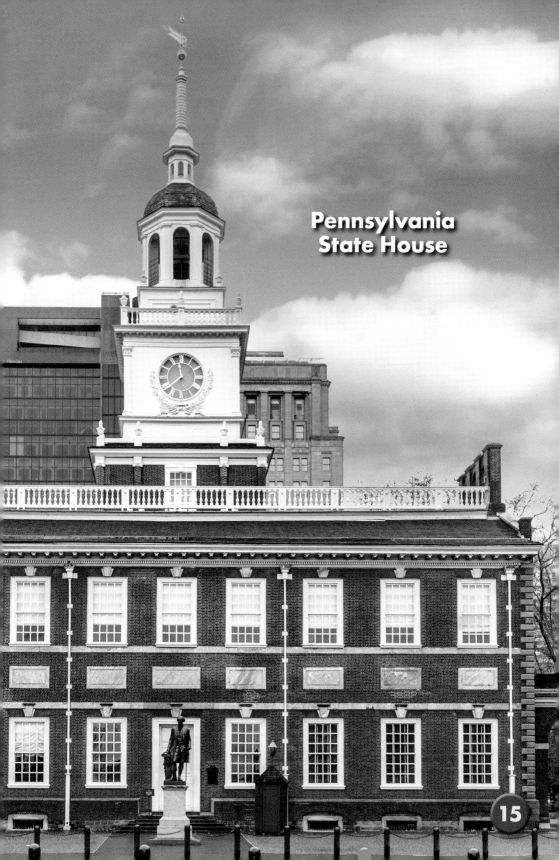

Pennsylvania State House

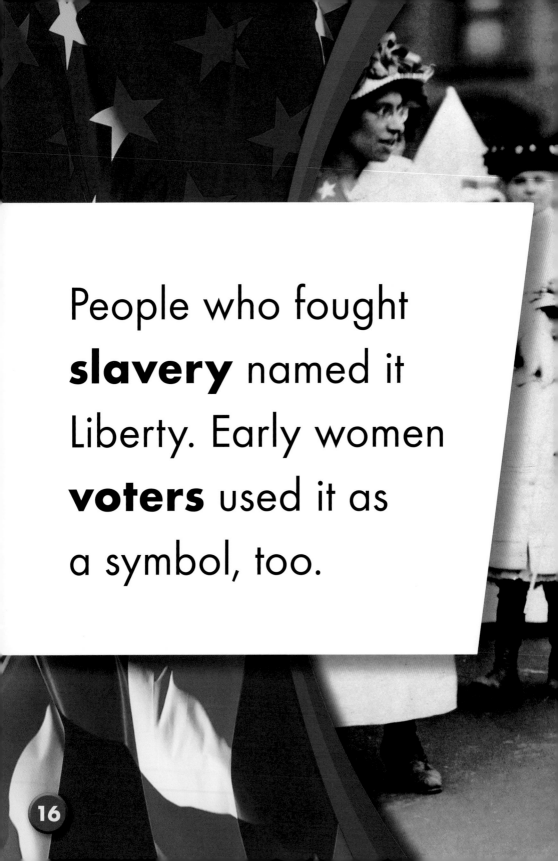

People who fought **slavery** named it Liberty. Early women **voters** used it as a symbol, too.

Today, people still seek freedom. The bell's message remains important.

The Liberty Bell
gives hope of
freedom for all!

Glossary

freedom

the state of being free

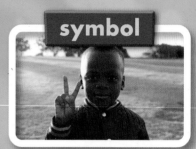

symbol

something that stands for something else

legend

a popular story from the past that cannot be proven true

voters

people who make their wish or choice known

slavery

the practice of owning people who work for no money

To Learn More

AT THE LIBRARY

Bailey, R.J. *Liberty Bell*. Minneapolis, Minn.: Bullfrog Books, 2017.

Gaspar, Joe. *The Liberty Bell*. New York, N.Y.: PowerKids Press, 2014.

Shamir, Ruby. *What's the Big Deal About Freedom*. New York, N.Y.: Philomel Books, LLC, 2017.

ON THE WEB
Learning more about the Liberty Bell is as easy as 1, 2, 3.

1. Go to www.factsurfer.com.

2. Enter "Liberty Bell" into the search box.

3. Click the "Surf" button and you will see a list of related web sites.

With factsurfer.com, finding more information is just a click away.

Index

The images in this book are reproduced through the courtesy of: f11photo, front cover, pp. 5, 6-7, 20-21; Tashka, pp. 3, 7; Matt Rourke/ AP Images, pp. 8-9; Library of Congress/ Getty, pp. 10-11; 3LH, pp. 12-13; Diego Grandi, pp. 14-15; IanDagnall Computing/ Alamy, pp. 16-17; Richard Levine/ Alamy, pp. 18-19; Everett Historical, p. 22 (bottom left); Monkey Business Images, p. 22 (top right); Burlingham, p. 22 (middle right); fstop123, p. 22 (top left); George Rudy, p. 22 (middle left).